Pearl Harbor Child

A Child's View of Pearl Harbor -
from Attack to Peace

by
Dorinda Makanaōnalani
Stagner Nicholson

designed by
Larry Nicholson

Concept and design by Larry Nicholson
Woodson House Publishing
P.O.Box 16536
Kansas City, MO 64133

Published by
Arizona Memorial Museum Association
#1 Arizona Memorial Place
Honolulu, Hawaii 96818

     First Printing, June 1993
     Second Printing, June 1994
     Third Printing, November 1995

Printed by Constable-Hodgins Printing, Inc.

ISBN 0-9631388-6-3

Printed in USA

DEDICATION...
Me ke aloha no

Dedicated with deepest aloha
to the memory of my mother,
Pansy Ka'ulaleianaikaohukalehua Akona,
and to her nine grandchildren.

Jeff (Makalapa)

Greg (Ka Leo)

Andy (Akona)

Ryan (Ka'ula)

Ishmael III (Ke Alii)

David (Ke Aloha)

Brandon (Ke Koa)

Sean (Ka U'i)

Carmael (Makanaōnalani)

Dorinda Makanaōnalani Stagner Nicholson

Acknowledgments

This book may never have gotten to press without the support of the Arizona Memorial Museum Association. I am indebted to Gary Beito, who brought the concept of <u>PEARL HARBOR CHILD</u> to the attention of the Association. It was through his enthusiasm and encouragement and belief that my story needed to be told, that this book became a reality.

My appreciation also goes to those generous individuals who shared their personal photography collections: DeSoto Brown, Abel L. Dolim, and Senator Daniel K. Inouye. Photographs and/or historical props were also provided by the Hawai'i State Archives, Bishop Museum, U.S. Army Museum of Hawai'i, Hawai'i War Records Depository at the University of Hawai'i, with much help from James Cartwright, Johnson County Museum System, National Archives, and, of course, the USS Arizona Memorial Archives. Also, a note of thanks to Mom and Dad for taking many of the snapshots that found a home inside this book.

Finally, the person most responsible for the completion of this book is my husband, Larry. His creativity shines through in the illustrations, typesetting, editing, and the overall design. He was the one who spent many long and late hours molding my words and weaving illustrations onto the printed page. For his talents, his help, and his love, I am eternally grateful.

D.M.N.

Contents

Preface: A Pearl Harbor Legend, *"The Little Yellow Shark"*   7

1 — My Family Moves to Pearl Harbor   11

2 — Sunday Morning, December 7, 1941   15

3 — December 8th: Confusion, Fear and No Information   23

4 — Where's My Dog?   25

5 — Adjusting to a New Life   27

6 — Hawai'i in the War Years   31

7 — Salvage, Victory Gardens and War Bonds   43

8 — The War Drags On   47

9 — Japanese-Americans in Hawai'i   51

10 — War is Over - Peace At Last!   55

11 — The Navy Takes Our Home   57

Area Map   60-61

Postscript   62

Guide — How to Say the Hawaiian Words in this Book   63

References/Credits   64

About the Author   Inside Back Cover

FOREWORD

December 7, 1941 is "a date that will live in infamy," according to President Roosevelt's famous speech. And it's true. Each year on that date, my thoughts always turn back to that incredible Sunday when bombs fell on Pearl Harbor.

I've been told (by someone in a national organization who should have known better) that I was too young to remember, that I couldn't have been a survivor of Pearl because there were no civilians living in the harbor, much less children. He was wrong; I was there.

On the 50th anniversary of the attack, I was invited to return to Hawaii as a speaker, to present a civilian's personal story from a child's point of view. In my preparation, I looked through many books on Pearl Harbor. Almost every publication had focused on the "military story" until recently, when two excellent books by Rodriggs and Brown arrived on the scene.

But not much has been written about **children** and Pearl Harbor, and what little I found had many misconceptions and downright errors which should be corrected. In making several presentations to audiences during the commemorative week, I found that people were eager to hear my story, and many wanted to know more than I could tell in a few minutes. So . . .

Yes, here's another book on Pearl Harbor. But I don't believe this story has been told before. To set the stage, let's begin with an old legend.

Preface: A Pearl Harbor Legend
The Little Yellow Shark *Ka'ehu iki manō o Pu'uloa*

*K*a'ehu was a little yellow shark whose home was in the clear and gentle waters of the Bay of Pu'uloa, known today as Pearl Harbor. The bay was a quiet, peaceful spot in those faraway days when only outrigger canoes were seen, and where the children of Hawai'i played along the shores.

Now, although Ka'ehu's family spoke of him as the little yellow shark, he was not so small. But he was called little because he was young in years. Yes, Ka'ehu was young and also strong, but he was also old with wisdom, for he was a descendant of the shark-god Kamailiili, who had given him wonderful magic powers and had made him very wise.

Ka'ehu had many friends and playmates in the big bay, but sometimes he was filled with longing for his childhood home off the Puna coast on the southern end of the big island of Hawai'i. One day he grew so homesick that he called his shark friends together and told them he was going back to visit his old home. They decided to go with him, and so began the journey from Pearl Harbor along the O'ahu shores to the open sea.

While swimming along outside the reef at Waikīkī, Ka'ehu and his friends met a shark visitor from Maui. His name was Pehu and he was a very different kind of shark from Ka'ehu and his friends.

*This Maui shark was dangerous, for he was a **Man-Eater!***

"Why do you swim in just one spot?" asked the little yellow shark although he knew the answer because he was so very wise. He knew that Pehu was eagerly waiting for some unsuspecting surfrider to come out far enough so that he might catch him and have a fine meal for himself.

"I am looking for a crab for my breakfast," Pehu coyly replied. Of course Ka'ehu knew the evil shark was not telling the truth, but he said in a friendly way, "We will help you catch your breakfast. You go and wait and hide yourself alongside the coral reef. My friends and I will go even farther out into the open sea. When the surfriders come, we will drive them toward the shore, and then you can easily catch what you call crab." This greatly pleased the Maui shark, so he went close to the reef and hid himself in its deep shadows.

Then Ka'ehu swam back to his friends and said, "We must destroy this man eater who will kill our good people. We will all go and push Pehu into the shallow water." Then he and his friends planned how they would save the surfers from the man-eating shark.

There were many surfriders laughing on their surfboards out in the surf, waiting for a rolling wave to ride into shore. Pehu called from his hiding place in the coral reef for the other sharks to come and help him capture his prize. But Ka'ehu called back, "Not yet! Not yet!

We must wait for a better chance!" Ka'ehu had his eyes on two men and the enormously high wave that was bringing them toward shore from out where the high surf begins.

Ka'ehu called, "Now!" as he signalled for his friends to help. Ka'ehu had planned that he and his shark friends would rush in under the enormous wave as it passed over Pehu, and move the men and their surfboards over to one side out of reach of the man-eating shark. And this is just what they did! As Pehu leaped to catch one of the men, the sharks hurled Pehu over the reef and into the shallow water. How they tossed him...over and over, until he plunged deeper and deeper into the sand and could not escape.

The surfriders hurried into shore and breathlessly told everyone what had happened, and that the evil shark who had been destroying some of their people was trapped in the shallow waters. They swam armed with sharp knives to destroy wicked Pehu. When they cut open his body, they found human hair and bones inside the man-eater, proof enough that this was the shark who had been killing some of their people.

The two men who had been surfing and had seen the wonderful feats of the other sharks now understood that the leader of them all was Ka'ehu, the little yellow shark from Pu'uloa or Pearl Harbor, whose ancestors were wise and kind and powerful. Ka'ehu loved the people of O'ahu and hated all evil which could harm them. The men knew then how he had banded together the other good sharks and had used the powers and wisdom given him by the great shark god Kamailiili.

When the body of Pehu was brought ashore, it was cut into pieces and put into baskets. The baskets were carried from Waikīkī to Pelelua, an ancient ceremonial spot, known today as where Nu'uanu and Beretania streets meet in downtown Honolulu.

A large area was cleared to build an immense imu, or oven. The Hawaiian chiefs and village peoples including the kei-ki (Hawaiian name for little children), gathered around the imu and when the fire was an angry red, in went the remains of wicked Pehu. They danced around the fire and chanted old me-le (Hawaiian legends and stories in song), in honor of the occasion where they no longer needed to fear the terrible man-eater. They also chanted their gratitude to Ka'ehu for his good deed. The celebration lasted until the imu fire was nothing but ashes.

All those who saw or heard that the man-eating shark had been captured and killed, knew that it was because of Ka'ehu's cleverness and his love for the people of O'ahu. They never forgot the little yellow shark who lived in the blue waters of Pu'uloa, and how he had saved them!

Author's note:
The hole in the coral reef off Waikīkī where evil Pehu was trapped? It is still known today to many of the old time Hawaiian fishermen.

My Family Moves to Pearl Harbor

1

How I would beg for "Just one more story, please Mom! One more Hawaiian legend, please?" I loved the ones about the fire goddess Pele and her youngest sister Hi'iaka, and especially those about Laka, the hula goddess. Mom was a kumu hula (teacher of Hawaiian dance) and so I often asked her about hula legends and any others that she would tell me.

One day, she told me the legend of the Little Yellow Shark that lived in the Bay of Pu'uloa. She also told me about the shark goddess, Ka'ahupahau, who lived in the same bay full of pearl oysters which is called Pearl Harbor. That's when I first learned that we would be moving to the Pearl City peninsula, a small strip of land surrounded on three sides by the waters of the Bay of Pu'uloa, better known as Pearl Harbor.

Our house was at 443 Jean Street in the area called Pearl City Peninsula. It was so close to the harbor that Mom could walk to her new job at the Pan American World Airways Clipper Base. She could come home on work days for lunch with my baby brother, Ishmael and our dog, Hula Girl. I was away in kindergarten at Sacred Hearts Convent, and Dad was at work at the Honolulu Post Office. The year was 1940.

Mom, Dad, Ishmael and me in our new front yard on the Pearl City Peninsula.

Passenger service began in 1936, when Pan American Airways flew their famous China Clippers directly into Pearl Harbor. The flight from California took more than 21 hours. The Clippers tied up at a dock just a short distance from our home.

Mom and Dad, all dressed up to greet visitors from the Mainland

In those days, children and their parents who came to Hawai'i by airplane flew directly to Pearl Harbor's waters and landed right on the water in a seaplane. The seaplanes, called "China Clippers," looked like flying boats, with four enormous propellers. After the seaplane landed, it would taxi up to a pier just like a motor boat. It would anchor just like a boat, and the passengers would get off onto a rough wooden dock. Mom could clearly see the seaplanes in the harbor from her desk in the library of the Pan American World Airways offices.

To be a child of the harbor was special. My friends and I would take our nets down to the piers where the airplanes were moored, and drop them into the shiny water to catch crabs. The best bait was fish heads, and we tied them to the center of the circular net to lure the crabs. I wanted the best bait, aku heads, so I could attract the most crabs, and especially Samoan crabs, which were the largest of all.

In the fall of 1941, I began first grade at Sacred Hearts Convent in Nu'uanu. But I wouldn't finish out the year there, because of events that were beyond my control, even beyond imagining!

The Japanese carrier Akagi, flagship of Vice Admiral Nagumo, on its way to attack Pearl Harbor. In the foreground, a crewman rests under the wing of a Mitsubishi Zero fighter.

The Zero fighter A1-101 (right background) was the aircraft flown by Lt.Commander Shigeru Itaya, who led the Akagi aircraft to Pearl Harbor. Note the heavy protective covering on the ship's tower.

Meanwhile, somewhere in the Pacific Ocean, the ships of Japanese Admiral Nagumo's Kido Butai (striking force) were making their way eastward through heavy weather and tossing wintry seas toward the Hawaiian Islands.

13

Three Nakajima torpedo bombers respond to "TORA! TORA! TORA!" the Japanese code words meaning the secret attack was a total surprise to the unsuspecting American fleet.

In that armada, four aircraft carriers would provide a portable airfield for 350 bombers, torpedo planes and Zero fighters. Their deadly mission—to attack the American fleet, peacefully anchored in Pearl Harbor a few hundred yards from my home!

Sunday morning, December 7, 1941

2

It was Sunday morning and Mom had the radio going. It was a large radio that stood on the floor, with big round knobs that had to be turned to change stations. The music played softly in the living room as Mom began to slice some papaya fruit for breakfast. We could hear the radio from our kitchen table as we sat down to eat our breakfast of Portugese sausage with rice and eggs.

We were not the only ones listening to radio station KGMB's soft music. The station had stayed on the air all night to provide a beacon to help guide a squadron of our B-17 Flying Fortresses as they flew across 2500 miles of ocean from California.

But still another group of planes used the radio broadcast to find their way to the islands. The station unknowingly acted as a guide to two groups of heavily armed planes with red circles on their wings as they flew from the Japanese carriers to execute their surprise attack.

Suddenly we heard the sound of low flying planes, then almost immediately, loud explosions, followed by more planes passing directly over our house. The blasts were too much for my impulsive Scotch-Irish father to ignore. He bolted up from the kitchen table and darted into the front yard. I was right behind him.

ATTACK

We shielded our eyes from the early morning sun and looked up into the orange-red emblem of the Rising Sun. The planes were so low, just barely above the roof tops, that we could see the pilots' faces and even the goggles that covered their eyes.

In the movies, an airplane attack always has the rat-tat-tat of guns as the plane dive-bombs its target. But when these Japanese planes flew directly over us, the sound of the bullets was muffled by the roar of the engines. Even though we couldn't hear them, the incendiary bullets found their targets. Our kitchen was now on fire and parts of the roof were gone. The front door of our next door neighbor was so bullet- ridden from the strafing that it fell from its hinges.

From our end of the peninsula we could see the old battlewagon Utah as it turned on its side in the murky water. Everywhere we looked there was smoke and fire. The odor of burning oil hung over the harbor. All these unbelievable sights and sounds and smells stunned my senses.

I remember the worried expression on my dad's face as he surveyed the chaos around us, and yelled, "Get in the car! We've got to get away from the harbor!"

But as we tried to get into our car, military police in jeeps shouted at everyone to get all civilian cars off the street immediately, driving them up into yards if necessary. We could soon see why, as truckloads of service-men tore by us trying desperately to get to their posts. Many of the men were still dressing, pulling on their pants or shirts or shoes, some even hanging out the tail gate.

The program on the radio was interrupted with dramatic news: "Air raid - Pearl Harbor! This is no maneuver! This is the real McCoy!" This message was later followed by an urgent order for all medical and military personnel to report to the hospitals and bases.

Dad still wanted us to get away, and so Mom, Dad, my baby brother and I piled into our old black Ford, not knowing where we were trying to go, but realizing that we had to find someplace to hide. Dad managed to drive around to another nearby vantage point on the harbor, and what we saw will never be forgotten.

One battleship was upside down and others were ablaze and helpless. We knew that countless men were dying out there. It seemed as if the water was on fire with burning oil. Overhead, we saw a lone Japanese plane calmly make pass after pass through clouds of black smoke rising from the disabled ships. Years later, when photographs of the attack were recovered from Japan, Dad and I looked at the photos and wondered—had they been taken from that plane? We think so.

Battleship Row. Small craft and fireboat assist USS West Virginia in fighting fires. USS Tennessee in the background.

The initial shock of that awful scene was soon replaced with waves of anxiety and panic sweeping over us, and we decided to return home. Dad drove back down the road to the Pearl City peninsula where we were stopped by military police. In the midst of great confusion and panic, they were in no mood to be cooperative.

Raising their guns, they screamed at us, "Get out of here! You can't go home—it's too dangerous! Find someplace else to stay!"

Not knowing what else to do, Dad turned around and drove our black sedan up Waimano Home Road to the sugarcane fields in the hills above Pearl Harbor.

Smoke billows from the USS Arizona. Just ahead of her is the sinking USS West Virginia (far left) and the slightly damaged USS Tennessee (left).

WATCHING THE BATTLESHIPS BURN

From the cane fields, we could see the harbor on fire. But most important, we could watch the skies, and if the Japanese planes came back, we could hide ourselves in the tall sugarcane stalks.

But I wasn't thinking about the dive bombers returning. I was thinking about my dog, Hula Girl. She was a black and white mixture, the kind of dog known in Hawai'i as a "poi-dog." I knew she was scared with all of the noisy blasts and explosions, and probably was hiding under my bed. Who was going to feed her and tell her not to be afraid?

Soon our neighbors from Pearl City began to join us in the cane fields. For a little while I forgot about not being able to go home to my dog, because some of my playmates had joined us. As children sometimes do, we forgot about the crisis for awhile. We enjoyed playing, while our parents worried about what to do.

We began to chase each other in and out of the sugarcane stalks laughing and talking. Our only concern was to be careful around the cane, as the leaves sometimes caused itching and you could get small cuts if you weren't careful. For a time, we didn't notice our worried parents, and how they all huddled together talking very seriously while we were busy playing hide and seek.

Our group in the cane field continued to grow. As each car arrived, all the adults rushed up, begging for the latest information. Finally, one of our neighbors joined us with some news.

He said, "I was listening to the radio. Just before noon, Governor Poindexter came on and declared a state of emergency. He said that Hawai'i was to be under martial law, meaning that the military was in charge. Then the Governor ordered all radio stations off the air in case the Japanese came back and tried to use the signals to guide them to the islands for another attack."

We drove our old Ford into the sugarcane fields. It was the only place we could think of to hide.

Our neighbor paused, and then continued. "Then my radio went silent. After that, military police with loudspeakers ordered all civilians on the peninsula to immediately get away from Pearl Harbor, so I came up here."

The Hawaiian sun was now straight up in the sky, and children in the canefields became bored with the games and began to cry. Most of us were hungry. I thought of the unfinished breakfast we left on the kitchen table earlier in the morning. The bananas and papaya would really be o-no (delicious) right now. Maybe my poi-dog Hula Girl had gotten so hungry, that she had gotten the breakfast food. That would be great. But what if she had been hit by a bomb or a bullet? It was then for the first time that I began to cry.

We could still see the smoke from the burning ships in the harbor as we looked down from our hiding place in the mountains. Some of the children slept in the back seat of cars, or on blankets placed on the ground. I sat on the hood of our car with my parents nearby as we continued to watch the harbor burn. I was fine because I was with my parents. With them, I was not afraid.

The grown-ups looked very serious and confused. Unanswered questions flew from their lips. How long were we to stay in the cane fields? What is happening in Honolulu? Have the Japanese forces landed yet? Have they attacked any of the other islands? Will the bombers come back?

If only there was some news to tell us what had happened, and what we were supposed to do! Someone had a shortwave radio, and the adults hovered over it. But there was still no reliable or official information.

After delivering their bombs, Nakajima Torpedo bombers leave Pearl Harbor and return to the Japanese carriers waiting for them at sea north of Hawaii.

We had been attacked, but were we at war? We knew we could not go back to our homes in the harbor. We were refugees. Would we hide in the cane fields and wait for the Japanese attackers to return?

From our vantage point in the cane fields, we kept a watchful eye on the harbor as it continued to burn, sometimes with flames shooting high into the sky as ammunition exploded, followed by another plume of dark, billowy smoke. As the sun dropped closer to the Waianae mountains and we reconciled ourselves to staying in the fields, military police found us. Again, they firmly told us we couldn't go home, and evacuated us to the recreation hall of a sugar mill at Waipahu about ten miles away.

EVACUATION TO A SUGAR MILL

The recreation hall was a small wooden structure that sat on a hill next to the sugar mill. There was a small soup kitchen and one bathroom. Approximately 100 civilian men, women, and children had been brought there. We slept on the floor.

That long night, sitting in total darkness, not knowing whether our homes had been destroyed, or if friends and family were all right, was hard to bear. Telephones were not to be used; they were only for vital military use. Mothers held their children close to them, and people were very gentle and soft-spoken with one another. Always, people took turns trying to get anything on the shortwave radio that would give some news about what was going on.

Then, suddenly, the silence was broken. It sounded as if every available gun on O'ahu had begun firing all at once. We had been told to expect the Japanese back, and this time they would invade. We really thought this was it—the expected invasion!

Red streaks in the night sky came flashing over Pearl Harbor, with sounds of gunfire from all directions. Who was shooting? Had the enemy returned to strike again? What was happening? From Waipahu, we saw the sky light up like an extended lightning storm. Then there was silence. A final question came to us out of the darkness: Had the Japanese landed?

The remainder of the night was spent in fear, wondering what the latest exchange of gunfire meant. The radio was silent, so we had no information. The phones were still restricted to official military use, so we couldn't call anyone to let them know we were safely out of the harbor. There was nothing to do but huddle together in the dark, draw our families close to us, wait for morning, and quietly ponder the unforgettable events of December 7, 1941.

December 8th:
Confusion, Fear and No Information

3

T he smoke from the harbor was clearly visible as my parents strained to see out in the early light. Many hours after the actual attack, we heard occasional sounds of exploding shells, caused when ammunition stored on the battered ships ignited.

Confusion, uncertainty, and fear were on my parents' faces. The radio had been left on all night for any tiny bit of information. The only real news was instructions for all vital personnel to report to work; everyone else was to stay off the streets. Those with medical, military, and government jobs were considered vital. My Dad was a government postal worker at the Honolulu post office near the Iolani Palace. So he reported to work, as did several other fathers from the evacuation center.

Families had little choice when spouses went to work. They simply waited, and hoped for a safe return.

The radio continued to be our lifeline. Everyone in Hawai'i gathered around radios, starved for any information. In the hall, we clustered around a small radio and listened to President Roosevelt broadcast his famous "Day of Infamy" speech that described the attack and asked Congress to declare war against Japan.

Damage was not confined to the military areas of Oahu. Sadly, the damage in Honolulu was the result of our own stray anti-aircraft shells, rather than enemy fire.

The next few days were spent playing with other children from the Pearl City Peninsula, waiting for parents to return in the evening with news of what was happening. Dad brought a newspaper, but with martial law and the need to keep any useful news from the enemy, the newspaper was heavily censored.

This was a time of rumors and misinformation. No one seemed to have good, reliable information. As a result, people were nervous and upset. Guards were posted everywhere, and if anything suspicious happened, jumpy trigger fingers were ready to fire.

A tragic example of this lack of communication and jumpiness had occurred the night of December 7th. The "Fighting Six," a group of our own fighter planes from the aircraft carrier Enterprise, were trying to land on the island. Sadly, our own overly-nervous troops mistook them for the enemy, and fired at them. This was the cause of the battle sounds and red streaks in the sky we had watched from the evacuation hall. That night, we lost five fighter planes and three pilots from the unfortunate "friendly fire." One of the "Fighting Six" crashed into the Palm Lodge, a small hotel just a block from our home, killing the pilot.

Above Left: Newspapers all over the world screamed news of the attack.
Left: Three civilians were accidentally killed in this car by "friendly fire," some eight miles from Pearl Harbor.

Where's My Dog?

4

After four or five days of sleeping on the floor at the sugar mill, the Pearl City evacuees were allowed to return home. At last, that meant I could see my dog, Hula Girl again. I couldn't wait.

As we came up our street, I remember peering ahead to see if our house was still there. It was! I was out of the car calling for Hula Girl before Dad even turned off the motor. My parents scurried around to see how much damage had been done, but I went looking everywhere for my dog. Our yard was full of shrapnel and when I couldn't find her, I just knew she had been injured by one of those jagged pieces of metal, and had crawled off somewhere to die.

I searched and called for her for the rest of the day. Dad tried to tell me that she was probably very frightened and was hiding somewhere. He assured me that she would come back very soon. With tears running down my face I kept looking. Up and down the streets I called for her. I even climbed up in the huge mango tree to see if I could see further and yell louder so she could hear me above the house tops. I finally had to come in when it was too dark to keep looking any longer.

Even though it was wonderful to be back in my own bed with sheets and pillows, I could not be consoled. Nothing else mattered to me if I didn't have my dog. She had been my constant companion ever since I could remember.

Mom had me take hula classes when I barely started to toddle, and Hula Girl would come along with us. Then, when Mom began teaching hula in our living room, I'd watch the classes with Hula Girl right at my side. I had given her that name because when she saw me, her happy tail would wag so fast that it made her hips wiggle in her own version of a fast hula dance.

As I lay in my bed, I thought I heard her whimpering under my bed. Quickly, I dropped to the floor and looked under the bed, but it was only my wishful thinking. But soon I heard the whimper again. If it wasn't under my bed - but sounded like it - it could only be from one place. Calling my Dad and grabbing a flashlight, we darted out the front screen door, down the few steps, and looked under the house.

Somehow, when I looked before, I had missed seeing her in that small, dark space. (Homes in Hawai'i don't have basements, and ours was a typical house which sat on short 18-inch stilts leaving just enough room for a crawl space.)

It was a miracle! Hula Girl was there and still alive. She was weak, but strong enough to wag her short tail a couple of twitches. We had a joyous, tearful reunion.

This photo was taken several years later, but still shows the crawl space under our house where Hula Girl hid during the bombing.

Adjusting to a New Life

5

With Hula Girl at my side, my friends and I spent the next few days playing as if it were summer break time. All schools were closed immediately, and mine was converted into a military hospital. Schools remained closed until February of 1942, almost two months later, so we had many play hours while Hawai'i prepared itself for an expected invasion from Japan.

I watched Mom fill up our bathtub with water, but not to take a bath. She was preparing us in case our water supply was cut off. Some of the rumors said that our water supply might even become poisoned. Mom stayed home with us a lot because her job at Pan American was on hold. The giant sea clipper planes could no longer land in Pearl Harbor. Since the attack, only military aircraft were allowed there.

Many of our play days were spent taking a basket and picking up pieces of shrapnel and seeing who could collect the most. I collected small bullet casings that made a high-pitched whistle sound when you blew on the open end. We also found many bomb casings, and used one for a doorstop for the front door all through the war and afterward.

The bomb casing we picked up in our front yard was used for a doorstop all through the war. One day, we noticed it was missing; someone had stolen it! The Hale Momi sign is for Mom's hula studio. It means "House of Pearl."

In the months following the attack, we often walked down to the tip of the peninsula for a closer look at the battleship Utah capsized in the harbor. It is still there today, just around Ford Island from the USS Arizona. The Utah has 58 men entombed in her hull, while the Arizona lost 1,177 men, most of them still aboard their ship.

The USS Utah capsized just off Ford Island. The USS Raleigh is in the distance.

Today, both are memorials to the men who died there. The USS Arizona allows visitors to come on board its memorial, and nearly 2 million do so each year to pay their respect.

The USS Arizona, as it looked after the fires were out, resting in 40 feet of water. Years later, the Memorial was built directly over her submerged hull.

Dad kept finding bullets in the walls of our house, especially the kitchen. These were incendiary bullets that were supposed to burn when hitting a target. Parts of our kitchen did catch on fire, and the blackened streaks were how we could tell the path of the bullets and where they had stopped. I still have a bullet that dad cut out of the wall above the phone with his pocket knife.

Dad spent long hours at the post office. One of his jobs was working with the mail that was salvaged from the Arizona and Oklahoma battleships. The salvaged mail was brought by the Navy to two big rooms in the Federal building, where about a dozen people sorted it. Not only was this mail wet, some of it was also burned. Dad and the other postal workers searched the damaged mail for names and addresses, trying to find enough information to send those letters where they were supposed to go.

This Japanese bullet was lodged in the wall of our kitchen. Mom carried this bullet in her coin purse for the rest of her life. It is the only one I still have of the many that struck our house.

FOOD BECOMES SCARCE

We had two grocery stores in our area. If there was any panic after the bombing, it was over food. Everyone was concerned, because the ships that brought food from the mainland might not be able to come, and supplies could be cut off completely. Lines formed at grocery stores and people tried to buy everything. To avoid a mob, only a few people would be let in the store at a time, and then sometimes only if the storeowners knew you and your family. This was a "special" kind of rationing that began even before the official ration stamps were printed and in use.

Next, the military governor immediately urged all non-essential civilians to leave. This meant everyone who did not have a job crucial to the war effort. The reason? Fewer mouths to feed, and fewer people to defend when the enemy returned. The wives and children of the military were forced to leave. Residents could stay or go. Some of my friends at school were sent to the mainland to live with family until the war was over. But the islands were home to my Hawaiian mother, and she couldn't bear to leave. We chose to stay.

Since much of Hawai'i's food must be imported, people were very worried. Long lines became an overnight fact of life, even for barefoot kids and poi-dogs.

Immediately after Pearl Harbor, the steamship lines were swamped with people who wanted to leave Hawai'i and return to the mainland.

Hawai'i in the War Years

6

All of Hawai'i prepared for the time when the Japanese would return and attempt to occupy the islands with their troops. There weren't enough soldiers to do everything in the frantic rush to protect the islands, so everyone—children, moms, dads— thousands of civilians all pitched in to help. One of the first requirements from the military rule was that everyone over six years old had to be fingerprinted and carry an I.D. card at all times. Schoolteachers helped by going door to door, since school was called off for weeks while the islands geared up for war. My Mom and Dad never did tell me that not only was the identification card to keep out enemy saboteurs, but it was to identify the body in case of bombing raids.

The effects of the war were seen everywhere, including barb wire on Waikīkī Beach.

UGLY BARBED WIRE AND DINGY BOMB SHELTERS

One of the first tasks was to clear land and put up barbed wire all around the island coast line. Even our famous Waikīkī beach had rolls and rolls of ugly barbed wire stretched across the sand leading to the ocean.

For protection against bombs and flying bullets, bomb shelters and

A new bomb shelter, clean and dry. They didn't stay that way very long.

trenches were constructed. These were especially important at schools. Our school had a bomb shelter, but most of us were scared to go inside because it was dark, smelled bad, and had bugs. One day at school, the air raid warnings sounded and we grabbed our gas masks and went dutifully to the air raid shelter. When we got there, it had filled with water from a rain the night before. We all cheered when we didn't have to go inside.

The military government demanded that each house build its own shelter. I remember my dad trying to dig a shelter for us in our back yard. He got his shovel and started scooping out the dirt. Living in the middle of a harbor, our dirt was mostly sandy and marsh-like. So dad only dug about ten shovels full before the hole filled up with water. We never did have our very own bomb shelter and I was glad. There was no way I was going down into those dark, damp holes, bullets or not.

CAMOUFLAGE AND BAYONETS

I did like the lacy camouflage netting, however. We had a lot of it on the Pearl City Peninsula to cover up some of the military installations that had large artillery guns. The netting went over the tops of the huge guns and kept them hidden from the air. The fabric was dyed brown and green, and woven into a net which looked like trees, grass and dirt.

Seen from below, strips of fabric, attached to netting, helped conceal military objects and materials.

Even some buildings in downtown Honolulu were painted green and brown. But camouflage paint on the buildings didn't work as well. They still looked like buildings, but with funny colors on them. Sand bags were placed in front of several, with soldiers standing guard with rifles and bayonets.

The bayonets always terrified me. I never even looked at the soldier's faces. All I could see was the sharp point of the knife on the end of the long gun. I knew that these were American soldiers, on my side, and there to protect me, but it didn't matter.

Above: Sandbags and bayonets in downtown Honolulu.
Right: Structures like the Aloha Tower were too large to be hidden under camouflage nets, so they were painted with irregular patterns in an attempt to make them less visible from the air. During the war, women joined the armed forces in record numbers.

When my school became a military hospital, I went to a school in downtown Honolulu next to the Governor's home. At the entrance to the governor's home were two soldiers with the largest bayonets I had ever seen. These were the two that I feared the most. Every day before and after school, I would cross the street and walk a block out of my way just to avoid looking or even coming close to those guns armed with their long, sharp knife blades.

GAS MASKS

Hawai'i was worried about the use of poison gas by Japan, and so every person in the islands was issued a gas mask. They were to be carried everywhere at all times.

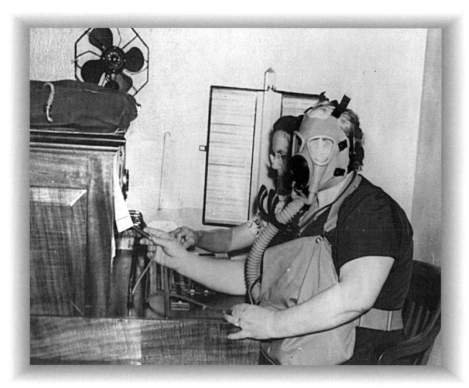

Even the telephone operators were issued gas masks, but I don't know how often they wore them. I suspect this operator just put hers on for the picture.

Mine felt heavy across my left shoulder in its brown canvas bag. My brother was only two, and his mask was almost as long as he was. Even babies had to have them. The infant version was really comical. It was actually a bag to slip into, with big bunny ears on top for decoration and a see-through window to look out of. Most of the mothers complained that their babies were afraid to be put into them. Mom said it made her very sad to watch me trudge off to school carrying my gas mask.

To be sure that everyone knew what to do in case of an attack, and to give emergency crews a chance to practice, regular drills were conducted. My Mom and Dad were air raid wardens and guided the drills with make-believe bomb bursts. My favorite part was to be a make-believe "casualty," stretched out on the side of the road waiting for a volunteer ambulance crew to find me and bandage my "injuries."

MONEY

Hawai'i was always preparing for the Japanese to return. If that occurred, the enemy would quickly seize the banks and use the American money to buy weapons or goods in other countries. To protect against that possibility, Mom and Dad, and all other Hawai'i residents, had to take their money and turn it into the bank. The bank replaced it with special currency that had "Hawaii" overprinted on both sides. This was the only legal tender for the islands during most of the war.

Above: My brother Ish and I, obeying the wartime rules to always carry our gas masks. *Below*: During the war, all paper money had "Hawaii" printed on it.

BLACKOUTS AND CURFEWS

Even the blackouts were fun - at first. We could have no lights on after dark, and it was fun to figure out how to eat in the dark when you couldn't see your food or anyone at the table. How we would rush to get everything done before dark! At first, it meant taking my flashlight into the closet and looking at picture books or listening to the radio while in there. That was an adventure, until it also meant there was nothing else to do but go to bed when it got dark. That's when I decided it wasn't fun anymore.

Before long, Mom and Dad, like all our neighbors, bought some black enamel paint and painted our windows black. Some people used black tar paper to cover their windows. Then we could turn our lights on, but with the windows and doors closed up, it became very stuffy. We weren't among the lucky ones who had an electric fan before the war, and it was impossible to get one after the war started. Boy, was it sticky and hot!

We had to be extremely careful about any light escaping from our house, because the block warden was very strict. If he saw any light, he would report it to soldiers in a patrol car. They took care of the problem by simply shooting out the light!

One time, Mom was rushing to get the wash done on the back porch with the aid of a flashlight. She was there just long enough to put a load into our old-fashioned wringer washing machine. But she wasn't quick enough, and the warden appeared, demanded that she turn off the flashlight, and threatened to take her immediately to military court. Several of our neighbors had been taken to court, sentenced and fined for just a

... after dark during the war.

Can you imagine how dark it would be with no street lights, no lighted signs on buildings, no lights in homes and no car lights? That's right, no car lights either. In addition to blackouts, there were strict curfews. No one could be on the streets after dark without a special pass. If you had a pass, you could be out after dark, but your car lights had to have a hood over them to cover most of the light.

My Dad had a pass to be on the street after dark because his job at the postoffice required him to work long hours. Our Ford sedan's headlights had a shield over them that looked to me like the eyes of a sleepy cat with eyelashes.

Dad was stopped many times when out at night, sometimes by military police, and sometimes by a volunteer civil defense guard. One night when he tried to drive home, he was stopped three times and had to show his permit and identification card while the flashlight was aimed first at his face and then at the card, making sure he was the person on the permit.

A couple, who were among Mom and Dad's best friends, often came to visit us for Sunday dinner. We had to plan carefully for them to come early enough to get home before dark, or arrange for them to spend the night in our little two-bedroom house. One time, they didn't leave soon enough and it got dark before they could get home. They had to spend the night in their car, and finish their drive home when the sun came up the

Headlights of our '39 Ford Sedan had to be covered with a shield to force all the light downward. While Dad was photographing the car, he wanted me to get into the act.

Each car had its own headlight shield design. None of them were very attractive.

CENSORSHIP

Censorship was a fact of life during the war years, and because of the critical importance of Pearl Harbor to our armed forces, all types of communications were censored, including newspapers, magazines, radio broadcasts, and even the U.S. Mail. Part of my Dad's job during the early part of the war was to censor the civilian mail.

On the second floor of the Honolulu post office, hundreds of readers would censor the civilian mail, and ink out or cut out any parts that were judged to be unacceptable or hurtful to the war effort. The Army and Navy had censors of their own. The objective for both civilian and military censors was to prevent any important military-related facts from falling into Japanese hands.

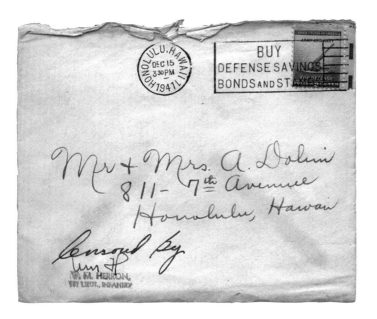

This letter was received by the Dolim family only a few days after the Pearl Harbor attack. Note that censorship was already in effect.

Strangely, one forbidden topic was the weather. If you mentioned the weather, it would be cut out of your letter. Even the newspapers could not mention forecasts or current weather, since this might help the enemy plan an attack.

Dad said that sometimes when a letter left the post office after the censors had finished with it, there were so many pieces cut out—that it looked like pieces of confetti in the envelope!

Above: This postcard, sent from Hawaii to New Jersey, shows the "passed" stamp applied by the censor. Below: On this card, the censor crudely marked through the names of the hotel and beach.

RATIONING

Across America, there were many shortages during the war. But in Hawai'i, we had shortages of **everything**! Rationing was the system used to deal with the problem. Rationing was a way to provide everyone with a fair share of things that were scarce. It was supposed to keep prices low, and make sure that people got what they needed. Since most products and supplies came to our islands by boat through possible enemy waters, the military had first priority on all goods.

One of the main shortages was gasoline. At first, gas rationing required coupons that were good for five gallons apiece, with a limit of two per month. The coupons were based on an A-B-C system with "A" being the lowest amount. Dad got a higher allotment because his post office job was considered vital, and he had to drive to work from Pearl City Peninsula to downtown Honolulu. There was a lettered sticker attached to his front windshield that dictated how much gas he could have. He had to turn in the required amount of coupons, which allowed him to purchase the gasoline. He and Mom spent many hours trying to carefully budget their use of coupons and the tiny ration stamps for the necessities of life.

Since coupons like these were needed to purchase gasoline, people could only buy a few gallons at a time, so they planned their driving very carefully.

Eggs were too expensive to buy, and even if you could find meat in the stores, it was also too expensive. That was when I first learned to like peanut butter, and beans, both foods that Dad introduced to our family. When we could get peanut butter, Dad would mix the oil off the top into the peanut mixture. At first I thought it was awful, like the beans he used to cook on the back of the kerosene stove. We ate a lot of beans with onions, and even a scrap of ham if we could get some.

Butter was scarce also. But we could sometimes get margarine. It came in a white sack with an orange-colored tablet. It was my job to take the white oleomargarine, put it in a bowl and mix in the orange tablet until it all became yellow. Later in the war, the tablet was replaced by a liquid in a plastic pouch, which made it easier to color the margarine to look like butter. Many Friday nights were spent around the kitchen table, kneading and mixing the white stuff into butter-looking stuff.

Many times, there was no toilet paper at the grocery stores. Just as the metal can of maple syrup shaped like a log cabin disappeared from the shelves, toilet paper was another of many things the stores couldn't keep in stock. Mom would save paper, usually newspaper, and rub it back and forth against itself to soften it, and that became our toilet paper. There was no way you could call it toilet tissue.

Across America, children and their families had to deal with shortages, and ration books became a way of life.

Mom and her lady friends couldn't get hosiery to wear on their legs for dress-up occasions. They were called silk stockings then. Her friends would put makeup on their legs to make them look like they were wearing silk stockings. Then they would draw a seam line up the back of their legs, because all hose then had seams. But Mom's legs were naturally brown, so she didn't have to paint her legs.

We all had to get used to doing with less of what was considered non-essential. But, like most kids, I missed candy and stuff with sugar, and you know what I missed the most? It was gum! Especially bubble gum.

Seamed stockings like these were very fashionable in the 1940's. The only problem was, you couldn't get them during the war, because nylon was needed for military uses such as parachutes.

Salvage, Victory Gardens and War Bonds

7

Our armed forces needed huge amounts of metal and rubber for planes, tanks, and ships. It was difficult to get rubber because the Japanese were patrolling the Pacific Ocean, cutting America off from rubber supplies in Asia. So, everyone was asked to gather and turn in any kind of rubber as a contribution to the war effort.

Hawaii's children, as well as mainland children, went door to door collecting what we could for rubber salvage. We gathered old tires, along with shoe heels, toys, sink stoppers, and even old bathing caps.

These Hawai'i Scouts are doing their part by collecting old tires to be recycled for use on combat vehicles.

Above: When America went to war, women workers were needed everywhere to help in the defense effort. No longer doing "women's work," many became experts at building tanks, ships, and airplanes. **Right:** *Children all over the USA collected scrap metal, including everything from old appliances to tin cans to pots and pans, as did these students at Kapalama School.*

Metal salvage included appliances, tin cans, pots and pans, anything that contained some metal. We even saved every bit of tin foil from gum wrappers when we were lucky enough to get some gum. We took each piece of foil and rolled it into a ball. As we added each new piece, we had a larger and larger ball to donate for the war. One friend said she knew that her ball of tin foil was going to be made into the bullet that would win the war.

VICTORY GARDENS

With the warm weather of the islands, and scarce supplies that must come by boat, Hawai'i was already well on its way to Victory Gardens before the mainland joined in. Children worked in the gardens alongside the whole family, planting vegetables. There were large community gardens in parks, vacant lots, churches, anywhere there was an unused plot of ground. People with a small amount of land just piled dirt on top of their air raid shelters to make room to grow their food.

We had enough room in our back yard to grow many different kinds of vegetables. My job was to hoe the weeds, and I hated it. I complained, and when that didn't work, I pouted. When I pouted, I wasn't allowed to go to the Saturday afternoon movie, which was our major form of entertainment in those days.

Because we also had a meat shortage, my dad said we were going to grow another crop that he called, "Pearl City Chicken." Calling it that was just to fool me, because he knew that I would eat chickens, but not what he really had planned. Without saying much, Dad built wooden cages above the ground, called hutches. After that, he bought some rabbits, and I eventually learned that they were to be a new food source for the family. But not for me!

Civilians who didn't have garden space combined their efforts in community gardens like this one.

The rabbits were an Angora breed with lots of fluffy fur. I named the first one, "Patches," and called his mate, "Mrs. Patches." I also named all of their babies. Loudly I would plead with daddy, begging him not to kill the rabbits for food. You can probably guess what happened next.

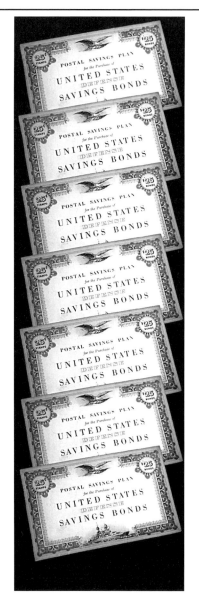

To save the rabbits, I began to hoe the garden, and pull the weeds without complaining. And I even learned to like vegetables.

WAR BONDS

The war effort needed great sums of money to pay for the increasing cost of the war. War bonds were used to raise money for the guns, bombs and bullets. A war bond was a special savings account. In effect, the people were loaning money to our country, to be paid back later with interest. Hawaiians were unusually patriotic, and in every sale of war bonds, we exceeded the goal set by the government .

War bonds were sold everywhere—in stores, post offices, door to door, and even along the sidewalks. If you somehow managed to avoid buying one, you would likely receive one for your birthday or Christmas.

The way Hawaii's children helped with bonds was by buying individual saving stamps, which went into a special book. I bought 10 cent stamps to lick and stick in my stamp book. I would go without lunch to buy the stamps, until I had filled my book with $18.75 in stamps, ready to take to the post office to trade for my war bond. By buying a few stamps at a time, even children like myself could help.

Based on population, War Bond purchases in Hawai'i were the highest in the nation, and consistently exceeded sales goals set by the government.

The War Drags On

8

With each passing year, more and more military personnel came to the islands. They were either on their way to battle, or returning, injured, to recuperate in Hawaii's hospitals. Eventually, the armed forces population on my island of O'ahu outnumbered the civilian population. There were men (many of them still looked like boys) in uniform everywhere.

My Mom, like other island mothers, was afraid for her daughter to be around so many men. I was not allowed to be anywhere near the section of Honolulu called the "Hotel Street" area. I couldn't even ride a bus through that part of the city because she didn't want me to see all the bars, tattoo shops, and honky-tonk photo shops.

The Hotel Street area was a major attraction for off-duty servicemen.

Mom had always been a working mother, with a job away from home. This was unusual for the 1940's, when most moms stayed at home with their children. But after Pearl Harbor, when the men went to war, the women went to work, and the government encouraged them to do so. It was common for women to work at jobs that previously only men had held. So Mom joined other working mothers, and also worked many hours overtime daily. Then she came home and taught her hula classes, and still tried to take care of my brother and me. It was difficult, but that's the way most families lived during the war years.

Other evidence that we were at war came from posters that were seen everywhere. They warned us about enemy spies, and urged us to support the war effort. There was no escape from the reality of wartime at movie theaters either. The newsreels were always about the war. Often, the cartoon characters were in the Army or Navy, and were doing their part against the enemy. Even the main feature would often have a war theme, as well as the comedies, which were supposed to make us laugh.

War Posters-Left above: Symbol of the importance of women in the war effort. **Left below:** A stern Uncle Sam promoted security . **Left:** A 48-star American flag urged us to work even harder.

Morale could be a problem. Everyone needed to be cheered up occasionally. The movies were a good way to do that, and on some Saturday nights there would be live entertainment after the main feature. Mom's hula students, known as the Hale Momi girls, which included me as the littlest dancer, entertained at some of the programs. I loved to dance, especially when wearing my favorite hula costume, a holoku. This is a long fitted dress, that flows out into a train like a wedding dress. Fresh flower leis matched the colors in our holoku. I also loved to wear a flower in my hair, even though it kept sliding off. I especially liked the holoku ever since my hula skirt fell off when I was trying to dance in Mom's show at the Lalani Hawaiian Village in Waikiki when I was barely three.

Local entertainers couldn't handle all the demand for shows, and so the U.S.O. came to the islands. One even came to my school. They sang songs like, "Praise the Lord and Pass the Ammunition." I remember trying to figure out how the U.S.O. showgirls got their eyelids to be blue. I had never seen blue eyelids before, and I thought they were so glamorous.

The United Service Organization (USO), mostly volunteers, provided recreation facilities for American troops and gave them "a home away from home."

| Jimmy Wilbert | Dorinda (me) | KaNani Austen | Lydia Hironaka | LaVerne Blackburn | Pansy (Mom) |

Part of the Hale Momi dance troupe, all dressed up to present "Pearl City Frolic" at the Princess Theater. Mom's troupe, like others, entertained often during the war.

Some of my friends were jealous that U.S.O. shows didn't come to their schools because they had school in private homes, usually on the front porch. But their jealousy was a small matter. Another problem was far more serious.

You see, these friends were of Japanese ancestry. Their small, one-story wood house had a special banner in the window. The banner displayed a gold star for their son, who was killed while serving the Army in Europe. This young man had joined the U.S. Army and served with the colorful 442nd Regiment from Hawai'i, which is a story in itself.

A "Star in the Window" was a symbol of great respect, indicating that someone who lived in this house was either in military service or had died in service for his or her country.

Japanese-Americans in Hawai'i 9

Many people don't know what happened to the Japanese-Americans who were already living in Hawai'i at the time of the Pearl Harbor attack. Within a week after December 7th, about 300 of them were sent to a detention camp on Sand Island, not far from the Honolulu airport. Eventually, over 1,400 local Japanese were isolated there. Many were sent to the mainland, to be held there against their will.

Sand Island, in the Honolulu harbor, is where many Japanese-Americans (along with a small number of European-born suspects) were forced to move after the Pearl Harbor attack. A small "city" of tents and cots was quickly built to house them.

Fortunately, the bulk of the Japanese-American citizens of Hawai'i escaped being sent to these prison camps, because it was impossible to isolate about 150,000 people living on several islands. There simply wasn't room to do that. Unfortunately, the Japanese-Americans living on the mainland, numbering more than 120,000, were not so lucky. They didn't have thousands of miles of Pacific Ocean to keep them from a prison camp, and many of them lost everything they owned.

Finally, after more than 50 years, some Japanese-Americans have received an official apology from the U.S. Government, and money to help make up for the treatment they received. Sadly, many have died through the years without knowing that one day the great error would be recognized. Some of their children took the letter of apology to the graves of their parents to show that at last, the government had admitted its mistake.

Senator Daniel Inouye, a former member of the 442nd Regiment from Hawai'i, was pleased with the final outcome.

"When Congress passed the Reparations Bill, this was a proud day for America. It takes a big country to admit wrong. Many countries would not do this."

> Daniel K. Inouye
> U.S. Senator from Hawai'i

Even though many of the island Japanese weren't imprisoned, they still faced a difficult and frightening time. Suspicion and outright hatred were sometimes directed at them. A few changed their last names. Many of them Americanized their first names. For example, my friend Eiko changed her name to Eileen.

Many of the island Japanese wanted to prove their loyalty to America, the country they had accepted as their own. Even though they had been born in Hawai'i and were U.S. citizens, there was much concern over

Above: Senator Daniel K. Inouye is a former member of the 442nd Combat Group, whose slogan, "Go For Broke" is island pidgin (slang) which means something like, "you can do it." Below: Inouye in his Army uniform on patrol in the mountains of Italy, where the "fighting 442nd" made a distinguished contribution to our war effort in Europe.

where their true loyalties lay. At first, when Japanese-Americans wanted to enlist in the armed services, they were not accepted. To prove their loyalty, some became volunteers who did hard manual labor for the Army. But it wasn't until January, 1943, before any were accepted. They quickly made up for lost time.

General Mark Clark reviews the 442nd. The extraordinary toughness, discipline and motivation of this unit made believers out of those who had doubted their loyalty and ability.

THE FIGHTING 442ND REGIMENT

Over 9,500 AJA's (Americans of Japanese Ancestry) volunteered for the Army, and about 2,700 were accepted. To avoid the confusion of Japanese-Americans fighting against Japan, these new volunteers were trained to fight against America's other major enemy in World War II, the Nazi's. Thousands of people turned out to cheer the new recruits when they sailed from the islands to fight in Europe. They served as the 442nd Regiment, and by the end of the war were honored as the most decorated unit in the entire American army.

The Famed 100th Battalion of the 442nd Regiment passes the reviewing stand at Kapi'olani Park.

The men of the Fighting 442nd had proven their loyalty!

Other Japanese-Americans did also. In fact, as early as January, 1942, a Honolulu newspaper stated that no espionage could be traced to the local population. Later, an FBI agent was quoted as saying he found the vast majority of the island Japanese to be loyal, honest, and hard-working citizens.

War is Over - Peace At Last!

10

Through the long war years, Mom continued to teach her hula classes at our home, and graduated many students at her yearly u-ni-ki (recital). By now, her hula classes also included wives and women stationed with the military at Pearl Harbor. In 1945, our military forces finally decided to end the blackouts and curfews, so each weekday evening she taught her students, very precisely, the graceful art of hula.

Mom thought we should cancel hula class the day of August 14, 1945. The news had just come that Japan had agreed to surrender, and she thought that her teenage students wouldn't want to come to lessons. But she was wrong. They wanted to come and be together that night. We had class, and then it was time for Mom to drive one of her students home. As we began our drive back through Pearl City, just as our car passed the courthouse, crowds of our friends and some neighbors surrounded all the cars on the road.

Suddenly, firecrackers exploded all around us. At first, it scared me, thinking that our car would catch on fire. But we were safe. People were just letting off steam. Mom sounded her horn, and we inched our way through the ecstatic celebration. Our neighbors paraded through the streets, banging pots and pans together and chanting, "The war is over." We drove farther down the peninsula until we could see the fireworks from the harbor, and hear the air raid sirens wailing along with the gas alarm gongs and whistles from the ships.

The sky over the harbor was flashing brightly with flares, each one adding its note in a symphony of light. The air was filled with all variety of ship's whistles adding their voices to the sirens and gongs in an unforgettable scene. In a spontaneous eruption of joy and excitement, people hugged and kissed anyone close to them.

Our old black Ford inched through the crowds, and slowly came down Lehua Avenue, making a right turn into our street. As we came closer to the house, our car lights picked up the white uniform of a sailor standing in a yard across the street. Unlike the others, he was alone. I watched him curiously, wondering why he wasn't with the jubilant crowds nearby. Then I saw that he had his own way to express his joy at America's victory. He leaned against a palm tree with his elbow bent, and rested his face in the crook of his arm. I didn't hear him cry, but I could see his shoulders and head quake with emotion.

The war was over.

Above: Staff Sgt. Michael S. Padeken of the 442nd Combat Team is joyously welcomed home by his family. Below: American servicemen celebrate VJ-Day in downtown Honolulu.

The Navy Takes Our Home

11

I was almost ten when the war ended. I thought our family could always live in Pearl Harbor, but it was not to be. We tried very hard to keep our home, but now that the fighting was over, the Navy could concentrate on moving the civilian locals out of the harbor. My Dad formed the Pearl City Peninsula Association, to join with our neighbors to see if we could keep from losing our land. The association wrote letters to the newspapers about the United States Navy intimidating ordinary working people who were natives of the islands, and stealing our homes.

We put up a long, hard fight, but all civilian property was condemned on the peninsula. We had to sign our deed over to the Navy, and then were required to pay rent. By this time, most of our neighbors gave up and left. Some took their houses with them. One of my last memories of Jean Street was our Filipino neighbor's house, cut in two like a deli sandwich, being towed down our street away from the harbor.

Most all of the original houses are gone now, except for one or two exceptional residences near the old Pan American pier which appear to be used for officer housing. It's difficult to tell where most of the old streets were, now that the multi-unit military housing has disguised the land.

Below: On one trip I took my two oldest sons, Jeff and Greg, to show them where I played on this pier when I was "a child of the harbor."
Below right: Just a few yards away is the marker showing where the China Clippers used to land.

This place is full of memories for me. A marker on one of the piers commemorates the landing of the first Pan American Clipper plane after its 21-hour and 20 minute flight from California on November 22,1935.

Close by is another marker noting that a midget Japanese submarine had also shared the harbor, but on a secret, deadly mission, six years later.

This is the same pier where I spent many hours with my crab nets. Further along the coastline, I could show you where the old Palms Hotel stood before it burned in the fiery crash of the American fighter plane which was mistakenly shot down by our own guns on the evening of December 7, 1941.

I could tell you as the child who will always remember the day when the bombs fell.

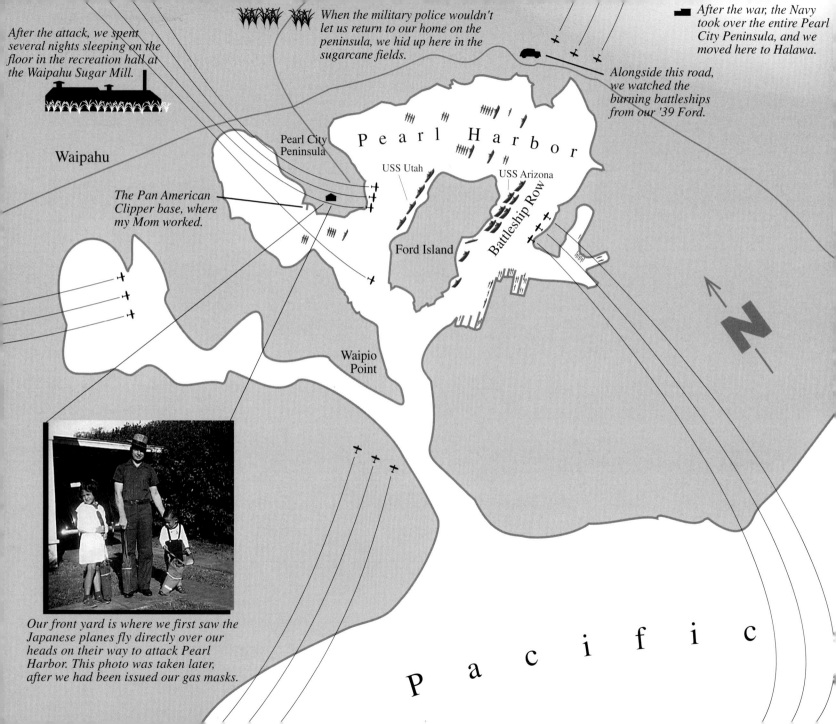

After the attack, we spent several nights sleeping on the floor in the recreation hall at the Waipahu Sugar Mill.

When the military police wouldn't let us return to our home on the peninsula, we hid up here in the sugarcane fields.

After the war, the Navy took over the entire Pearl City Peninsula, and we moved here to Halawa.

Alongside this road, we watched the burning battleships from our '39 Ford.

Waipahu

Pearl City Peninsula

The Pan American Clipper base, where my Mom worked.

P e a r l   H a r b o r

USS Utah

USS Arizona

Ford Island

Battleship Row

Waipio Point

N

Our front yard is where we first saw the Japanese planes fly directly over our heads on their way to attack Pearl Harbor. This photo was taken later, after we had been issued our gas masks.

P a c i f i c

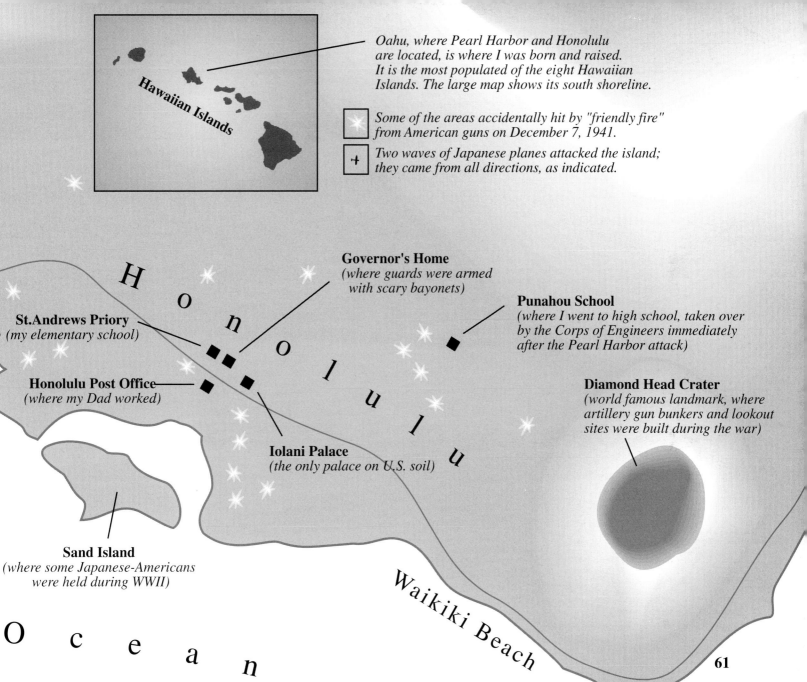

Hawaiian Islands

Oahu, where Pearl Harbor and Honolulu
are located, is where I was born and raised.
It is the most populated of the eight Hawaiian
Islands. The large map shows its south shoreline.

Some of the areas accidentally hit by "friendly fire"
from American guns on December 7, 1941.

Two waves of Japanese planes attacked the island;
they came from all directions, as indicated.

Governor's Home
*(where guards were armed
with scary bayonets)*

Punahou School
*(where I went to high school, taken over
by the Corps of Engineers immediately
after the Pearl Harbor attack)*

St. Andrews Priory
(my elementary school)

Honolulu Post Office
(where my Dad worked)

Diamond Head Crater
*(world famous landmark, where
artillery gun bunkers and lookout
sites were built during the war)*

H o n o l u l u

Iolani Palace
(the only palace on U.S. soil)

Sand Island
*(where some Japanese-Americans
were held during WWII)*

O c e a n

Waikiki Beach

Postscript

Dad and I, pictured in 1991 at his apartment near Kansas City, where we prepared the anniversary talks we would give in Hawaii on December 7th of that year. Dad died July 8, 1995.

We were able to live as civilians in the harbor for more than ten years after the war began. When forced to move, and still feeling our connection to the harbor, we moved up to Halawa Heights, on an overlook where we could always see the harbor, although from quite a distance.

One day not long ago, after spending many years living on the mainland, I returned with my husband and sons to revisit Pearl Harbor and the Pearl City Peninsula, and walk the streets where I had grown up.

It wasn't easy to do, because the Navy still controls the area, and access is severely restricted. At first, I tried explaining to the military police that we only wished to make a brief visit to my childhood home. They were not impressed, and wouldn't allow us to proceed. Then we sought help from a family friend, a retired Navy officer, who personally took us to the peninsula with him. Then, at last, it was possible to re-visit the places I've described, and share them with my family. The feelings that were experienced during that visit have now come full circle in this book.

Thank you for letting me share them with you.

How to Say the Hawaiian Words in this Book

There are only 13 letters in the Hawaiian alphabet—the five vowels, and eight consonants. All words and syllables end with a vowel, and no two consonants may be placed together. The result is almost musical, and many people find it quite beautiful.

Divided to show the syllables	How to say the word	Divided to show the syllables	How to say the word
Ha-la-wa	*Hah-lah-vah*	La-ka	*Lah-kah*
Ha-le Mo-mi	*Hah-lay Mo-mee*	Le-hu-a	*Lay-hu-ah*
Ha-wai-'i	*Hah-wy-ee*	Ma-ka-na-o-na-la-ni	*Ma-ka-na-o-na-la-nee*
Hi-'i-a-ka	*Hee-ee-ah-ka*	Mau-i	*Mau-ee*
Ho-lo-ku	*Ho-low-koo*	Me-le	*Meh-leh*
Ho-no-lu-lu	*Ho-no-lu-lu*	Nu-'u-a-nu	*Nu-u-ah-nu*
I-ki Mano	*Ee-kee Mah-noh*	O-'a-hu	*Oh-ah-hu*
I-mu	*Ee-mu*	O-no	*Oh-no*
Ka-'a-hu-pa-hau	*Kah-ah-hu-pa-how*	Pe-le	*Peh-leh*
Ka-'e-hu	*Kah-eh-hoo*	Pe-le-lu-a	*Peh-leh-lu-ah*
Kai-mu-ki	*Kye-mu-kee*	Pu-'u-lo-a	*Pu-u-loh-ah*
Ka-ma-i-li-i-li	*Kah-ma-ee-lee-ee-lee*	Pu-na	*Pu-nah*
Ka-pa-la-ma	*Kah-pah-lah-ma*	U-ni-ki	*Oo-nee-kee*
Ka-pi-o-la-ni	*Kah-pee-oh-lah-nee*	Wai-a-nae	*Wye-ah-nigh*
Kei-ki	*Kay-kee*	Wai-ma-no	*Wye-mah-noh*
Ku-mu	*Ku-mu*	Wai-pa-hu	*Wye-pah-hu*

References

Knudsen, Eric A. TELLER OF HAWAIIAN TALES, 1945, published by Coca-Cola Bottling Company, Honolulu, T.H. (out of print)

Credits—Photographs, illustrations, props

Author's Collection—Cover, Title Page, Dedication, 11, 12T, 12B, 19, 27, 35, 37T, 55T, 57

Bishop Museum—47

DeSoto Brown Collection—39T, 39B, 40

Abel L. Dolim Collection—13T, 13B, 14, 20, 38

Ken Hatfield, Lee's Summit Journal—62

Hawai'i State Archives—32T

Senator Daniel K. Inouye—52T, 52B, 53

Johnson County Museum System—15, 36, 46, 49B, 50

Rita Klepac—41

National Archives/Central Plains—44L, 48

Larry Nicholson—7, 8, 9, 10, 16, 21, 22, 25, 29, 46, 55B, 58L, 58R, 59, 60-61, Inside back cover

University of Hawai'i War Records Depository—24B, 30T, 30B, 33L, 34, 37B, 43, 44R, 45, 54, 56T, 56B

US Army—42

US Army Museum of Hawai'i—51

USS Arizona Memorial Archives—12T, 17, 18, 23, 28T, 28B, 31, 33R

Jim Wilbert Collection—49T